Understanding the Numbers

Make Your Business and Your Life Better

Nick Hixson FCA FCCA FAIA

INDIA · SINGAPORE · MALAYSIA

ISBN
Hardcase 979-8-89588-660-1
Paperback 979-8-89498-864-1

Disclaimer

This book has been prepared for information purposes only and is not intended to and should not be relied on for specific accounting, tax, legal or business advice. The author and all affiliates and related parties accept no responsibility for any losses that you may incur from acting upon the contents of this book. You should consult your own advisers, as they will be able to help you best with issues and advice specific to your circumstances. Advice before the event is better seen as an investment rather than a cost.

What Others Say

"Wow. It took me years of study to learn the invaluable lessons that this brilliant little book demystifies in minutes."

– Steve Pipe,
FCA – Former UK Entrepreneur of the Year

"This is the book that I wished someone had given me years ago! Management is about choices, and ultimately all of those choices are based upon what we find in the financial reports of the firm. Getting these right and relying upon them in key decision-making sessions is an absolute imperative for successful leadership. This book tells you how to do this!"

– Bill Fischer,
Senior Lecturer, Sloan School of Management, MIT; and Professor Emeritus of Innovation Management, IMD, Lausanne, Switzerland.

Contents

About the Author

Nick Hixson is a chartered and certified accountant in practice and has been working with small and medium-sized businesses for over 40 years. He has around 100 clients, mainly UK-based. He specialises in strategy, leadership and management for SMEs, helping them grow and be the best that they can be.

He is also an Associate of the Peter Drucker Society Europe, edits the Global Peter Drucker Forum blog, and is (2022) Chairman of the Advisory Board of the World Institute for Action Learning.

He writes blogs at www.hixsons.co.uk/support/blog on how SME business owners can think differently about their businesses and themselves to improve them both.

Introduction

I've worked with around one thousand small businesses over the last 40 years. I've seen a lot of owners make the same mistakes time and again because they struggle to understand the story of their business in numbers. Mistakes that have cost them time and money and a good deal of worry. I don't want this to happen to you.

So, I decided to write this book to help you understand your numbers and what you can do to make your business and your life better.

Purpose

Who is this book for? Small business owners like you need to know what changes happen in your business so that you can make better decisions. There is a language of numbers, which will tell you just about all you need to know if you learn it. But it's not like learning a language at school. It's much easier.

There is some use of technical terms, but just enough to grasp the basics. You don't have to be fluent; you just need to equip yourself with some ideas and principles.

This is not a primer in bookkeeping, so that you can do it all yourself. You have better things to do with your time.

It's about understanding the numbers, not doing them.

There are plenty of hints throughout that will make your business life easier and better.

Using this book, you will be able to make sense of the mass of numbers you come across in your business. Which ones should you concentrate on, and which should you safely ignore? There are several categories, some of which you will need to look at often and in detail, some you only need to look at occasionally, and some annually. And there are ones where you need to ask your accountant as they crop up so infrequently or are so unusual you'll forget about them.

Some of this you will know. Skip them and use the book as a manual to dip into when you need it.

Change Tactics

You need to understand the relationships between numbers and why if one number changes, then at least one other number in your business will, too.

You don't care about the process, but you do care about the result. To understand the result so that you can improve, it, needs some underlying knowledge and context. But not too much. It's not difficult, and quite often your knowledge of the business, coupled with the strong hints the numbers give you, will point you at a possible solution which you can test.

It's always advisable, when contemplating a decision, to ask your accountant first.

Apart from the wide business knowledge they have, they can also point out any regulatory issues, tax implications and any other areas that might be impacted. That's what you are paying them for. It's also cheaper in the long run to avoid failures by asking first. Think of the loss if it goes wrong and how hard you will have to work just to get back to your pre-decision days. I've seen too many small business owners forget to ask me first when they could have sense-checked their decision before wasting precious time and money.

You could look at **A list of common issues** section, rather than reading the whole book. But do read the **Decisions** section as these drive all the other elements in your business and this book.

Your Business

Always think in context. How does this relate to your business? What does your business do, and how does it do it? Do people pay you as you sell your goods or services, i.e. cash sales (cash, credit card, etc), or do they pay after a period of time, i.e. credit sales? Similarly, do you buy things and pay for them immediately, i.e. cash purchases (including cheque, credit card, debit card and cash), or do you pay for them later, i.e. credit purchases? Or do you do a bit of both?

Do you buy goods to resell? Do you work on the goods before you resell them, or do you simply sell them? Or is yours a service business where you sell your expertise?

Who are your customers? B2B (Business to Business) or B2C (Business to Consumer)?

Break your customers down by type, size, ease of doing business, etc. More details about that are in **Sales management.**

As a business owner, you must ensure that you have a high-level view of where the business is and where it is going. You also need a detailed view of the things you need to change. It is important that you have just enough information to decide whether you need more information. Only when you need more information, do you need to dive into the details. You should be able to see what you don't have to do, as well as what you do have to do.

A List of Common Issues and How to Fix Them

How do I…

Construct a **Business plan and forecast.**

Compile and manage **Business plans and forecasts.**

Check if I'm making enough money (**Reports**).

Make sure I'm not losing out on costs (see **Cost cutting, Fixed & variable, etc.**).

Make sure my customers are profitable (see **Pricing and Contribution, Reports**).

Make sure I'm charging enough (see **Setting prices**).

Make sure I won't run out of money (see **Working capital cycle**).

Make sure I don't get fined for late VAT, etc. (**Mechanise and clean up workflows**).

Make sure invoices go out promptly (see **Get paid on time**).

Adjust margins to make more money (see **All customers are not the same**)

Plan for my future by **Finding your True North?**

Check if my stock is turning over fast enough (see **Working capital cycle**).

Recognise when it's starting to go wrong (see **Reports**).

Make sure I've got enough reserves in case of a problem (see **Shareholders funds**).

Finding Your True North

Do we know our audience? Or do we jump from one thing to another, looking for the next big thing or the next deal because we are all in FOMO, fear of missing out? FOMO can lead to flirting with one thing and then another, never finishing any of them. Never getting what you want.

Don't run after everything. Decide on your market and what you are good at, and stick to it. Talk to those people and not any other people. Or, to quote an objective set by one of my clients, "I will stop marketing to people I complain about." Discover your True North and stick to it.

Nuclear loneliness leads to a lack of purpose

For 99% of the time homo sapiens have been on this planet, we have existed inside a community. No longer. Now there is nuclear loneliness, that feeling of thinking it is all down to you, no one to help, listen to you, empathise with you. The modern world gives us the ability to withdraw from it and hide behind our doors and computers. Added to that is the solitary existence of running your own business. Your ability to get fulfilment from what you do is dependent on others getting what they want first – your customers, people, suppliers. We don't function well in this state.

It doesn't have to be like this. Better to find a sense of belonging, to join and contribute to communities. We can all find a sense of purpose, belonging, and being valued by others.

Your True North

Finding our True North in business helps us decide what is important to us.

Ways of finding your True North are in Sam Coniff's book Be More Pirate. It investigates how pirates intentionally got bad press. There's an argument that the first brand wasn't Coca-Cola but the pirate flag – feared but universally recognised. As a piece of marketing it's brilliant.

Pirates had clear lines of democratic control, sharing of the loot, a system of healthcare, all enshrined in the Pirate Code, which, contrary to the movie Pirates of the Caribbean, weren't guidelines. There were elements of community in pirate life as well. The community of the ship, enshrined in the Code, and also the tribe of pirates collectively.

Each code was unique to each ship and expressed that what the pirates had agreed was fair. As such, it showed their purpose and values. It described their True North.

What is important to you?

I think it's about objectives. Businesses and academia tend to focus exclusively on business objectives. But it's really about what is important to you personally – your personal objectives.

Business objectives are only a subset of personal objectives

Personal objectives come first. It's the same principle as life-work balance instead of work-life balance. Surely we all want more life, not more work? And for certain, no one ever went to work to fulfil a business objective. They went to fulfil a personal one, which the business facilitated. Many personal goals are achieved through work, not by work.

I've had some interesting objectives set by clients. One was for him to spend more time with his father. He was aware that time was passing. Another couple wanted the opportunity to build family bonds over holidays (a small window of opportunity as the children grow up) and whose sales and profits have quadrupled in the last 5 years. Personal first – then make the business fit to you.

Do you want to find your True North? What speaks to you? Why is it important? You need to find ways to hold on to that and your place in your world. That way, you could be a bit more Pirate.

1

Decisions

You want to make better decisions and avoid bad ones. To be successful in business or in life, you don't have to be brilliant; you just have to avoid making big mistakes. Here's a tennis lesson to help you do that.

Do You Play to Win?

Professional tennis players are all very, very good. They play to win by manoeuvring their opponent around the court until they can put the ball out of his or her reach. It's a game of tiny margins and great accuracy.

Or lose?

Amateurs – same rules, same court, same equipment. But amateur players play to lose. They aren't very good. Mistakes are frequent.

To win, a player just has to be better at not losing than their opponent. The winner gets a higher score simply because the other player loses more points.

How do amateurs win?

So, if you are not very good at something, how do you win, either in tennis or in business? Assuming most of your competitors are similarly handicapped, you win by making fewer mistakes – avoiding stupidity.

In tennis, the strategy is to keep the ball in play and wait for your opponent to make a bad shot and win you the point. Years ago, I used to play tennis (badly) with my equally bad friend. I always won, even though our lack of ability was similar. At any time I was under pressure, I knew if I hit the ball straight at him (not hard!), he'd freeze, and his shot would go out.

Business is similar. Don't bother trying to be clever. Avoid mistakes – keep the ball in play. Your competitors, in trying too hard, may well slip up.

Take the quiz

This quiz was given to Warren Buffett and his friends by his mentor, Ben Graham.

Graham gave them 20 questions which could be answered true or false. He told Buffet that 10 were true and 10 were false. Most people got fewer than 10 correct. Think through how you would deal with it before you look at the answer at the bottom. It doesn't matter what the questions are. It's about how you deal with the problem.

The point Graham was making was that most of us try to play with professionals, but we are nearly all amateurs. If you play with the pros, you are playing with someone cleverer than you – you're playing in a rigged game. You need an edge.

Give yourself the edge – Invert the problem.

We need to give ourselves a better chance if we assume (usually rightly) that we are amateurs. We can do this by inverting the problem. It's a way of changing thinking away from our habitual thought processes, which can limit our opportunities to find new ways of dealing with an issue.

Inversion comes from a German mathematician, Carl Gustav Jacob Jacobi, who proposed that many hard problems are best solved if they are addressed backwards. This forces you to uncover hidden facets of the problem that you would otherwise not see. You need to address these issues forwards and backwards.

How to invert – an example

Innovation is vital to an organisation, and is mostly dealt with by finding all the ways innovation can be achieved. Instead, invert this and look for all the ways innovation is discouraged in your organisation. Eliminating these bad shots might allow innovation to flourish much more readily.

Thinking forward increases our chances of doing harm, whilst thinking backwards reduces it. It's your avoiding stupidity tool.

Quiz – The answer

The answer to do better than Buffett and his friends is to mark all the questions either all true or all false. That way, you would at least get 10 right. That's better than most of the very clever Buffett group.

Three steps solution

The moral of this tale is:

Assume you are an amateur.

Keep the ball in play – don't be too clever.

Invert problems to aid decisions

And just maybe this will improve your tennis as well.

Bookkeeping entries only record decisions that were taken earlier. Go back and reflect on this. ***Your books reflect the past, whereas you are interested in the future but can only act in the present.*** However, in reflecting on your past decisions, your books allow you to go back and do just that. Ask these questions:

What decision was it?

Who made the decision?

What information did I have to make it?

What information did I need?

Would I make the same decision now?

Curiosity – question everything: Who (should it be someone else), what, where (should it be somewhere else), when (should it have been at a different time), how (is there a better way), why…and should it have happened at all? And if it shouldn't have, how do you stop it from happening again? Perhaps **check your biases** and see if you leap to the **wrong conclusions**. We all do it at some point, so make sure you sense-check your decisions, and maybe **test that you aren't being overconfident.** Here's more on those 3 elements.

Check Your Biases

The defining role of a manager or business owner is to make decisions, and no matter how many books we read or courses we attend, we are all still prone to making poor decisions caused by our own innate ways of thinking.

This often occurs because we fool ourselves through our own psychology – it's called cognitive bias. This and the next few paragraphs will help alert you to the common ways in which we fool ourselves and how we can sense-check our decisions and make them just that little bit better.

Entrepreneurs are born optimists – they have to be. But they are often disappointed when the new product or service they launch, expecting marvellous results, disappoints. There has been an investment in time and money, which would not be made if only they knew then what they know now.

Overconfidence

We've already alluded to this. It's borne out of several aspects: the first is that our knowledge is limited to something new, and we don't know how limited it is. But we know we have to make a decision, even though we don't know what we don't know. Being optimistic means that we perceive risk differently – specifically, we perceive things to be less risky than they really are, and we do not easily measure risk accurately. Overconfidence also means that we tend to believe what we want to believe. We find a fact that supports our case and then try to find other facts that support the first one. It's hardly scientifically rigorous, but it's quick. And we have no time! So, we make a decision.

Remedying overconfidence

We can avoid these issues by making sure we check our facts and give due weight to all the facts we get, even if they do not support our case. Make sure you systematically gather information so that you know you have a broad base on which to make a decision. And also remember – particularly in the case of a new product or service – that sometimes the things you decide not to do make you wealthier than the things you do decide to do.

Confirmation bias

This follows very easily from the overconfidence element as we only look for things which we think will give us the result that we want. We don't look at statistics very thoroughly as we don't understand them. Avoid groupthink, as this is one of the remedies for confirmation bias, along with ensuring that you talk to a whole range of people who may not agree with you. Their insights might be just as valuable even though you may not want to hear them.

Gambler's fallacy

This is when we make a decision based on past events that has no bearing on the existing situation at all. A simple example is a coin toss. We toss the coin 10 times, and it comes down heads 7 out of 10. We might gamble that it will come down heads again – many people would. Statistically, the odds are 50-50 each time, so you should bet that way. We may assume that because our investment decisions have been good so far, our next decision should be equally good. It's an interesting use of logic! I have seen clients make that assumption incorrectly, and it has cost them dearly. They will assume that because they're good at their existing business that a new venture, which they know very little about, will be equally successful. It can take years to recover from that mistake.

Remedying the gambler's fallacy

Don't look chronologically, don't assume! Drill deep into the data and believe what you see so you don't just see what you want to see. Are there any patterns in the successful ventures you've done so far that are repeated or not in the next idea that you want to launch? Are those patterns valid in this new area?

Don't jump in – stop, reflect, ask other people, especially those with broad business knowledge. They can sense your ideas realistically to give you the best chance of success. They may see risks where you cannot. That's not being negative, it's being realistic. Optimists, remember (that is probably you), describe realists as pessimists.

Wrong conclusions

We've looked at some of the ways you can guard against your mind tricking you into making decisions that might come back to haunt you. Here, we will explore some more ways you can trip yourself up and what you can do to guard against them.

Anchoring

Anchors are usually useful – cues that enable us to run a quickly learned behaviour – see a red light and immediately start to brake. We haven't consciously thought about what to do, as often there's no need or no time. Note that this is learned, generally through repetition or a single important event.

However, an anchor can work against us, so we leap to conclusions when the underlying facts, whilst looking similar, are very different from the events that created the anchor.

We may act in haste only to repent at leisure. Anchors can also kick in when we are rushed and make a hasty choice based on a flawed view of the issue. And we all are rushed, most of the time. Or we have a first impression bias when we ascribe attributes and values to something or someone when a little more time might show us that our view is out of date.

Remedying wrong anchors

Firstly, do you have to decide? And if you do, do you have to do it now, or can it wait until you can devote some time to it?

Some decisions are made just to get them out of the way, as other imperatives are demanding of your time. And whilst you shouldn't put things off, you do need to take enough time to get it right. That old saying is a case in point – "There's never time to do it right, but there's always time to do it again." Make sure you make decisions once, and make sure you can live with them. Are the facts similar, or are you fooling yourself ? – stop and check your assumptions. It all takes time – we've dealt with that. It doesn't mean you have to go over every decision slowly, just…not so fast.

Fundamental attribution error

"It's Tom's fault – he should have known that would break!… If only the banks had lent me more!… If the Government hadn't changed the VAT rate, this never would have happened… The weather was against us – we thought it would be much warmer in January… We were just unlucky."

In other words, everyone else was to blame. Never you. The condition can produce a state of learned helplessness, where you think you can't improve your situation owing to outside forces.

Remedying attribution error

Check you've trained Tom properly – check that he understood, it's not enough that you have told him. Assume the banks won't lend all the time – have a plan if they don't. Stress test critical areas so that a change in VAT won't cripple you. Research weather patterns! Take charge!

More specifically, develop some more emotional intelligence – put yourself in the other person's shoes so you can anticipate events better. Don't stereotype – all bankers are…human beings just like you! Find out what makes them tick. Don't assume, as you will usually lose out.

Misused risks

In 1995, women in the UK were told that taking the contraceptive pill doubled the risk of thrombosis. It was calculated that information led to 13,000 extra abortions in England and Wales the following year. What nobody told women was that it doubled the risk from 1 in 7000 to 2 in 7000. One study showed that to most people, a 30% chance of rain tomorrow meant that it would rain for 30% of the time – wrong! (studies by Gerd Gigerenzer).

It's all about statistics and how you assess risk. Which we do generally via the mechanism of language, not mathematics. We are used to language – we use it all the time. If the risks are expressed mathematically, we would think a lot harder, and if we didn't understand, we probably wouldn't take the chance.

Check risk method

The pill issue was described as a relative risk – "it's doubled." Expressing it as an absolute risk changes our thinking completely – it's now 2 in 7000. Most people would think that was acceptable.

Try to express statistics in absolute terms, and again, that means stopping for a moment and asking yourself what is really meant. So, the next time you see "20% risk reduction," ask from what to what, before you take any action. If you want some entertaining practice, just watch the adverts on the TV. Most use relative risk measures. You will tune into what they are not saying quite quickly.

Gigerenzer also recommends that when you go to a restaurant, you don't ask the waiter what he recommends; ask him what he would eat! Hint – he knows his tastes, but not yours, so he will go with something very safe if you ask for a recommendation. What he eats is generally good. It may not be to your taste, but it will not be what the restaurant has that is going out of date or where they have bought too much and need to get it sold. And it makes for more exciting meals.

More on Overconfidence

"The first rule of the Dunning-Kruger club is that you don't know you are in the Dunning-Kruger club." We are all in it, says David Dunning, explaining the Dunning-Kruger effect, which is that people of low ability tend to overestimate their abilities.

Here's the classic graph, courtesy of the Journal of Personality and Social Psychology.

What does it mean for owner-managers?

Simply that when we are new to the task or have limited experience, we tend to overestimate our abilities. As we do not experience a stable environment in business for long, we are often in new environments where we have new tasks or limited experience. Consequently, we tend to operate on the assumption that we know more about the task than we actually do. And that has consequences for our decision-making and results.

Entrepreneurial hubris

We've mentioned before that entrepreneurs are naturally optimistic people. It's a necessary characteristic. But like all swords, this is a double-edged one. We need the optimism to be able to start new things, and push through barriers to reach our goals. However, optimism has to be tempered with some realism, and the Dunning-Kruger effect suggests that our view of realism may be overblown.

Consequential decisions

There are many instances where we have adequate experience and information. This is generally when we are doing something with which we have experience or where there are reasonable connections between our decision and our existing situation.

But consequential decisions are ones where we have new tasks to explore. These are the big decisions in our life and our business. Shall we start up in another town, shall we change our product line, shall we explore new markets? It's the equivalent of moving house, deciding to have children, or marrying. ***Whilst we can imagine the benefits, we can't really imagine the reality because we've never experienced it.***

It is these decisions that particularly need more care and the realisation that we may well overestimate our abilities.

Decision-making techniques

There are ways of dealing with this issue. These revolve around 3 separate areas:

a. facts or opinions

b. probabilities or certainties, and

c. questions.

Facts or opinions

You need to separate one from the other. Most beliefs we have are opinions, not facts. Facts can be checked, and simply saying, "I know this is true," does not make it so. Quite often, when we are asked in surveys about what we know to be true or not, people will always choose something rather than say, "I don't know," which is often the truthful answer to the question. Saying "I don't know" allows you to explore rather than decide too quickly. In many cases, "I don't know" is a very useful solution.

Probabilities or certainties

The confidence that entrepreneurs often feel leads them to describe future events as certainties when they are no such thing. Whilst it's helpful to have that drive and commitment, it is also helpful to recognise that what they are describing are probabilities – likelihoods of success. Assigning percentages to these events is a useful way of describing what you think might happen. It's also useful to remember that ***probabilities, if they are stacked, change their meaning***. Simply do the maths– if you are 80% certain that you will sell 100 new items, but it is dependent upon same-day delivery, a price point of £5, and 50 new customers, all of which are also 80% certain, then the overall chance of success is not 80% but just over 40% (0.8 x 0.8 x 0.8 x 0.8) – you have to multiply all the probabilities together. It tends to change your thinking when you do this!

Questions and naïve realism

Ask yourself, do I really know? Ask yourself, what could go wrong, and could you live with the consequences? Ask other people and question why they think the way they do. Their context will be different, and they should be able to provide you with a more rounded perspective. In particular, ask people who have different views than yours. Don't ask people with exactly the same experience and knowledge, as they are just going to agree with you, which will not help, and it might encourage you to do the wrong thing. You need a critical friend, not just a friend.

Finally, test your decision in a small way. Only jump in when you know the depth and temperature of the water. And ask yourself, where are you really on that graph?

Consider this extract from Rudyard Kipling's The Elephant's Child

Six Honest Serving Men

I keep six honest serving men

(They taught me all I knew);

Their names are What and Why and When

And How and Where and Who

It's all very well making a decision, but it has to be implemented effectively. These 6 questions give you a framework to see if your idea will be achieved. And they also help you analyse what has gone on in past decisions.

We also know that the world is changing very quickly, and an overreliance on past performance is not going to serve you well. However, what you can do from an analysis of the past is make inferences that you can test to see whether the decisions you made then are still valid now.

This is your main job. You have to make the time to do it. Do not spend all your time on the day-to-day tasks.

2

Relationships Between Elements of Your Business

Think about how elements interact with one another. Ask yourself if this, then what?

There are 2 sorts of relationships: functional relationships and mechanical relationships.

Functional relationships Examples include production and sales, labour and production, sales commission and sales, advertising and sales.

If one changes, you expect a predictable change in the other – so if you make one more item, you expect to sell one more item, etc.

Like this:

I sell 1 more unit for	£100
I bought it for	£60
I had to deliver it for	£2
I pay my salesperson commission of	£5
They had to make 5 sales calls, 2 in person for each sale	
(Expect telephone and motor expenses to rise)	£10

Common examples of the data and assumptions that drive functional relationships might be:

Gross profit %

Number of sales calls for one sale

Average order value

Lifetime value of customer

Customers pay on average after 30 days

You pay suppliers after 30 days

You need 60 days' sales in stock at any time

What are the **relationships** you expect in your business? Make a list, making sure you are clear what is data (facts), and which are assumptions. For example, you have always held 60 days' sales in stock, so you assume you have to. But times may have changed. Now map the relationships between them. You need to be crystal clear how these drive the business.

Relationships and Assumptions

The list above is a mixture of relationships and assumptions. Don't take them literally but recognise when you are making assumptions. Assumptions are based more on external behaviour – will customers pay after 30 days? Whereas functional relationships are based more on the internal business model, like this one: If you buy at £50 and sell at £100 then your gross profit is 50%.

Your sales price is your decision, but it is your customer's decision when you get paid.

Go back to your list and reflect on which of those are your decisions and which are outside forces, like customers and suppliers. And then check your books. Are you right? What can you do about it if you are wrong? You might end up with a table like this:

In the first line, relationships exist between sales (1), Cost of Sales (2), No of calls (3) and Average order value (4), and so on.

		Data/ Assumption	Internal/ External Decision	Relationship
1	Sales prices	D	I	2, 3, 4
2	Cost of Sales	D	E	1,3,4
3	No. of calls per sale	D		1,2
4	Average order value	D		1,2
5	Customers pay after 30 days	A	E	1, Cash flow
6	Pay suppliers 60 days	A	E	2, Cash flow
7	60 sales in stock	A	I	Cash flow

Break down the sales as above into their components to expose the relationships. There are plenty more – these are just a few. Plot all that you can, and you will understand better how they depend on one another and what that does to your bottom line and cash flow. Challenge all the assumptions. Is there a better way? Do you, for example, need to hold 60 days' sales in stock, or can you call stock off from your supplier when you need it? There's a lot of cash tied up in stock and debtors. It's useful to find ways of freeing that up. That can be internal, such as we've just discussed, or by refinancing to give you cash for growth. Business owners spend a lot of time on their **profit and loss**

accounts but much less on their **balance sheet**, where all the cash is locked up.

Breaking Down Changes in the Numbers

All sales and costs are a product of volume and price, even the telephone bill. Looking for changes can be masked by forgetting this. Look for those volume changes as well as the price. You are often stuck with the price, but you may be able to reduce the volume. You don't always have to literally calculate it – does it make sense from what you know has gone on in your business over that period? Only if it doesn't should you investigate. And then only if it's significant. Use your time where it's going to have the most impact.

Mechanical relationships – double-entry – the **4 rules of bookkeeping** are only a logic system. If it's this, then there must be that. The mechanics lead you to where the functional relationships are represented in your books. It's predictable, so that makes it much easier for you to see what's important and what isn't. Be sure that the entries are in the right place so that the relationships become clear. A decent bookkeeper is worth the investment, or you can use an online system and be consistent in making entries so that it will show things you may want to investigate. Get your accountant to regularly check your online books as well so that it saves you time and money at year-end and highlights any repeated mistakes, which also costs money to put right. And it helps you make better decisions.

3

Vocabulary

The language of numbers – basic vocabulary

It's important that you use the right words with the right meanings. So often, people say "me" or "my" when they mean their business or company, which runs by different rules muddling decisions. It isn't your money; it's the business's. It's important to get this right. Also, using the right terms helps give you clarity on what to do. There aren't many of them, so do take the trouble to read and refer to this section.

Bookkeeping is a double-entry method, so there are debits and credits. Debits go on the left, and credits on the right of the double-entry. There are only **4 rules of bookkeeping,** and the explanations below show whether you should normally expect a debit or a credit for each category.

Vocabulary mistakes

Because some words have 2 meanings or are used incorrectly, clarifying the correct meaning helps you to interpret what a word in your books means and therefore how it behaves. Beware of how you describe items so that you don't confuse yourself. Above all, be consistent.

Typical examples are:

Invoice – can be either a sales invoice that you give a customer, or a purchase invoice you get from a supplier.

Receipt – can be a receipt of money (as in from a customer) or a purchase invoice.

Payment – are you paying a supplier, an expense or being paid?

Balance Sheet

This shows what your business is worth and what it owes at any one point in time, called the **balance sheet date.** Usually, this is the end of the month, quarter or year.

Fixed Assets (Debits)

Like **Fixed costs** you should not monitor them because they change so infrequently and you already will have put some time into deciding what to buy or sell. Fixed assets are the assets that you own and use to produce the work that you do, so commonly things like machinery, motor vehicles, office equipment, buildings etc. You don't buy and sell them but need them to do the work that results in the buying and selling.

Current Assets (Debits)

Assets you own that are traded to make sales:

Stock (**Working capital**)

Debtors - Accounts Receivable (owed to you) (**Working Capital**)

Bank (if the bank owes you) (**Working Capital**)

Current Liabilities (Credits)

Trade creditors – Accounts Payable (people you owe) **(Working Capital)**

Bank (appears here if overdrawn, so not current assets)

Value Added Tax (VAT)

Payroll taxes (PAYE)

Tax – Corporation tax. Personal tax is not a business cost or liability.

Shareholders' Funds (Reserves)

This is the result of the Debits less the Credits – what the business is worth, in the simplest terms, at that time. This value won't be what you hope to sell the business for, as it doesn't usually include goodwill, but it's still good to track over time.

A very small value indicates that the business has few reserves so it might struggle to survive a setback, such as a competitor opening up nearby, ill health, a customer failing and owing the business a lot of money, a pandemic or some other unforeseen event. It's always good to retain some assets, usually bank based, in the business so it can carry on whilst you weather the storm.

How Much Should You Keep in Reserves?

It's OK to set a number (e.g., I need to keep £20,000 in the bank), but as the business grows over time, that target can become inadequate. Perhaps it is better to describe the amount you need as X months' overheads, both fixed and variable, plus what you need to live on (your drawings). Typically, this would be 3-6 months' overheads. That way, you won't keep building the reserves when you could be drawing more out to fulfil your personal goals without risk to the business.

Profit and Loss Account

This shows a period of time and the transactions in that period, be it a month, a year or some other period. It describes the buying and selling operations and the necessary costs (overheads) to achieve that.

Sales

Sales, Turnover, Receipts

Sales should always be considered as excluding VAT. VAT is only a collection mechanism for HM Revenue & Customs (HMRC). Whilst you get all the cash for the sale and the VAT into your bank, the VAT is HMRC's money, so we don't count it as sales. We add it to the VAT liability on the **balance sheet**.

What are the relationships? One relationship must be the quantity and the price of each category or sales item times the number of each you sell. Here's an example of what you might sell.

Item category	Price each	Quantity sold	Sales value
A	£10	100	1000
B	£6	200	1200
C	£8	50	400
D	£20	50	1000
		400	3600

Sell on credit or for cash – this is how the bookkeeping works with the debits and credits.

Sell on Credit	Debit (Dr)	Credit (CR)
You sell 10 items at £100 each ex VAT		
Sales (Ex Vat, Profit & loss account)		1000
Balance Sheet		
Debtors	1200	
VAT (owed to HMRC)		200
And when you get paid		
Bank	1200	
Debtors		1200
Sell for cash (immediate settlement) Sales		1000
Bank	1200	
VAT		200

Ways to Change Sales and Improve Cash

You can sell more things or sell at a higher price. How? You can read more about **14 ways to charge more** (below), which includes splitting bundles or taking components and creating a bundle. An example of a bundle is a mobile phone, earphones, and case bought together, which are cheaper than buying them separately. Your advantage is that you are making one larger sale and one delivery, so you should do better. Or sell the items separately but at slightly higher prices so that you are compensated for the extra effort of making multiple sales. You might offer both to give your customers maximum choice and give you maximum chance of a sale.

Case Study

You might also be able to buy back items and to sell an updated or better model, which a paddle board retailer did. They had a shortage of supply from China, so part-exchanged older cheap boards to buyers who wanted a better board. They then sold the part exchanges as well, but kept some for their paddleboarding school and rentals.

There are examples of changing sales prices and changing the **Cost of Sales** when **setting prices.**

14 Ways to Increase Prices Without Losing Customers

1. **Offer guarantees** – Customers will part with their money more readily and pay a higher price if they know that they can get their money back if something goes wrong.

2. **Provide sensational service** – Study after study has shown that customers are willing to pay more if you give them great service. Research also suggests that companies providing great service grow twice as fast as those with bad service.

3. **Make the price seem insignificant** – Perhaps by breaking it up into little bits and expressing it in terms of pence per day or pounds per usage. This "trick" is one of the keys to the success of the National Lottery – i.e., they have been able to persuade almost half the country to spend £100 a year by breaking the annual costs down into seemingly insignificant £1 tickets.

4. **Reduce discounts** – In many industries discounts off list prices are the largest single group of costs – and yet they are usually given with little or no senior management involvement or authorisation. Considerable savings can usually be made by tightening up discount authorisation procedures. Savings that lead directly to higher net prices and profits.

5. **Use creative discounting** – For example, replace flat rate discounts (e.g. "10% across the board") with stepped discounts (e.g. "5% on the first £1,000, 10% on sales above £1,000"). Not only do they look more impressive and encourage people to buy more, but they often also work out cheaper.

6. **Describe as investments** – Describing your price as an 'investment' rather than a cost can often go a long way towards persuading customers to buy.

7. **Less than expected** – Repeatedly tell your customers that you may have to put up prices by, say, 20% – but then only actually increase them by less than 20% (how far below 20% you pitch the eventual price rise should depend on your assessment of the true depth of their "horror" when you make the initial suggestion). By making the eventual price rise less painful than your customers were expecting, you can turn a potentially damaging increase into a triumphant success.

8. **Soften the blow** – Try to reduce the prices of some items in your range at the same time as increasing the prices of most other items so that you soften the bad news with some good news and make a point of dwelling on the latter.

9. **Explain why** – Be prepared to explain why prices have risen, perhaps because of cost increases, and point out that, had it not been for improvements in your own productivity and efficiency, the increase would have been even higher. Better still, explain that the price has increased due to improvements to the quality of the product. Emphasise the enhanced features, improved packaging, increased reliability, enhanced customer

support, faster and more convenient delivery and any other factors that make the product better and, therefore, worth paying more for.

10. **Justify your prices** – It is vital to have a strong justification and defence for your high prices prepared in advance. This is likely to include knowing the prices of your most expensive competition, demonstrating the savings and benefits from your product and demonstrating that your product is hugely superior and therefore slightly more expensive because... Do you have a set of written scripts to help you overcome price objections? And has every aspect of those scripts been tested to make sure that they are giving you the best possible results?

11. **Use "Non-price" increases** – For example, consider charging extra for installation, delivery, insurance, handling, storage, urgent orders or rapid delivery. You could also try increasing your minimum order size and introducing a surcharge for any orders below that threshold, revising your discount structure, slimming down the specification of your product and stripping out any expensive features that are of only limited value to the customer, and charging interest on overdue accounts.

12. **Change the package** – If a customer tries to knock you down on price, don't change the price; change the package. In other words, never simply crumble on price. Always trade a price reduction for some concession from the customer, e.g. a larger order or cash up-front.

13. **Trade for referrals** – If all else fails, you can always trade a one-off price cut for customer referrals.

14. **Top-down pricing** – Do you always show your customers the most expensive options first? Top-down pricing is a simple but highly effective way of increasing the amount customers spend.

Cost of Sales

Cost of Goods Sold, Contribution, Direct Costs

These are the costs directly associated with making your sales, so these are the things you buy to sell, the labour to make them (or salaries to make the sale), costs of transport to customers, subcontract costs, etc.

Cost of Sales traditionally meant the cost of the item that you have bought to sell, but now extends into salaries for service-based activities like professional services, digital agencies, etc, as salaries are the costs associated with earning the sale.

Examples

Your business sells temperature controllers. So, you need to buy in bulk wires, cases, dials, electronic components, etc. All these you make up into the items you sell.

Your business sells website design, hosting, and associated services. You buy internet domain hosting, apps to integrate into the website and your team spends time on designing and building the websites.

You sell domiciliary care services, where carers go to people's homes. Your Cost of Sales is the carers' wages, social security, pensions, and travel to customers.

Costs are excluding VAT. This is the reverse of the sales VAT mechanism. Whilst you pay out all the cash for the purchase and the VAT from your bank, the VAT is HMRC's money that you have paid via your suppliers, so we don't count it as a cost. It reduces the VAT liability (owed to HMRC) on the **balance sheet.** Here's an example of what you might buy.

Item category	Cost each	Number sold	Cost value
A	£5	100	500
B	£2.50	200	500
C	£3	50	150
D	£12	50	600
		400	1750

Buy on credit, or cash – this is how the bookkeeping works

	Debit	Credit
Buy on credit		
Cost of Sales (Ex VAT, Profit & loss account)	500	
All the rest of the entries are on the balance sheet		
Creditors		600
VAT (owed by HMRC)	100	

And when you pay your supplier

Bank							600
Creditors				600			

Buy goods and services for immediate settlement (bank transfer, debit card)

Cost of Sales/ expenses				500			
Bank							600
VAT				100			

Don't accept using the same suppliers year on year. Get a second source, ask for discounts for being a good customer, or for paying faster, or bulk orders etc.

Most of the control you can easily exercise is internal, not customer-driven.

This looks very similar to the description of how sales works above, because it is similar. The rules of double-entry work in reverse – you are incurring a cost and paying for it, instead of making a sale and getting paid.

Gross Profit

Gross profit or gross margin is the difference between what you sell something for and what you buy it for.

Item category	Sales value	Cost value	Gross profit (%)
A £10 each	1000	500	500 (50%)
B £6 each	1200	500	700 (58.3%)
C £8 each	400	150	250 (62.5%)
D £20 each	1000	600	400 (40%)
	3600	1750	1850 (51.4%)

It's interesting that the highest priced item, D, has the lowest % gross profit, whereas the lower priced items, B and C, have the highest. You need to keep in mind the margins as well as the sales value and the possibility that your higher ticket items might not be your route to success. It's unlikely that you will be able to sell only the higher margin products, especially if you want to sell complementary products (so buying A and C together for example). It's usually about the sales mix – the blend of sales of all your products and services that brings the best results. You need to be aware of what you are selling and how this might change over time. (see **reports**).

Case Study

A waste disposal company made its money by hauling waste from building sites and taking it to landfill, which it had to pay for the tipping charge. To expand, it needed expensive trucks and more drivers. To achieve adequate profits, the trucks had to be used a lot, so they needed regular maintenance, and some had breakdowns when they couldn't earn money.

The company changed its sales mix by building its own mini recycling plant, which cut down the amounts that were sent to landfills and sold the recycled waste as topsoil and bases for new builds. It reduced its overall sales but increased its gross profit by more, making better profits.

You can look at the overall **gross profit** and see it hasn't changed much over time and feel relieved. But you can see from the table, or you may know from your own business, that some of your products haven't been selling as well as before, so that is being masked by the overall result. To get to the same gross profit must mean that some other products are doing better and it may be that you can capitalise on that by focusing on those products.

Overheads (or Indirect costs)

Overheads are all the other costs apart from the Cost of Sales. It depends on your business's activity where some of your overheads lie. For example, power for your printing press would be the **Cost of Sales**, but light and heat for the office would be overhead and virtually fixed. Try to think of a fixed cost as being regular (e.g., rent every quarter) and changing a little, but not with activity levels. This isn't a strictly correct definition, but it will work well enough for you. There's no hard and fast rule, and don't try to over-analyse this. Give most of your attention to the costs that have relationships to sales.

Fixed Costs

Examples include:

Premises – rent, rates, water, insurance, heat and light (but power for your machinery might be Cost of Sales)

Salaries, pensions (unless production-based, in which case Cost of Sales)

Telephone, internet (usually, unless your business is a call centre or outbound sales, in which case it is Cost of Sales)

Professional fees

Post, stationery

All ex-VAT

Variable Costs (Incurred Regularly, Such as Monthly)

Examples include:

Commissions – directly related to sales

Motor and travel – may be related to sales in part, e.g. the salesperson's but not the director's

Telephone – may be related in part to sales, but may be relatively small so treat it as fixed.

An Example Showing Relationships between Sales and Costs Associated With the Sale

For every unit sold at £100, you incur Cost of Sales of £50, with a Gross Profit of £50.

But for each unit, you need to pay commission of 10%, and usually it takes on average 4 visits to a customer for the salesperson to make a sale, and literature and samples are needed.

The average order value is 100 units, so an average sale is £10,000. The 4 visits costs £50 each in motor expenses and the sales literature etc is another £60.

Whilst there is a clear relationship between sales, commission, and other expenses related to the sale, some of those expenses occur before the sale, in expectation of it. So, they may not relate to sales in the same period, but overall, the relationship will be valid.

If you are happy that the relationships are valid, you can plan for that. Also, you know that the proportions in any one period may not exactly fit the model, as costs are incurred prior to a sale. It's easy enough, if the figures look very wrong, to find out where potential sales are in the buying cycle so you can be comfortable that your model still works and that sales will flow as expected. And if not, you might want to change your model and sales forecast.

It would also be useful to see what the range of orders were to get to the £1000 average. You don't want to chase too many small orders, as they may need the same number of visits to land the sale. Your accounting software should be able to tell you this (see **reports**).

Again, remember that all figures are ex-VAT. Don't factor in cash that isn't yours, especially HMRC's.

Net Profit

Net profit comes after all costs, but before tax, dividends, and drawings. It shows what the business has made over the period being measured, be it a month, year or some other period.

Directors' remuneration or drawings. This is money you take to live on. Drawings is the term if you are a sole trader or a partner, and remuneration is if you are a director. Strictly, remuneration means salary and is taxed under PAYE and is an expense in the Profit & Loss Account, but most small business owners take what they need as a mixture of salary and dividends, the dividends being treated like drawings, with no tax relief.

4 rules of bookkeeping

1. **Balance Sheet items.** Assets are debits (left-hand column), liabilities are credits (right-hand column)

Like this	Debit (Dr)	Credit (Cr)
Fixed assets	X	
Stock/Work in progress	X	
Debtors	X	
Bank (the bank owes you)	X	
Bank (you owe the bank)		X
Trade creditors		X
Payroll taxes owed		X
VAT		X
Hire purchase and loans		X

2. **Profit & Loss account items.** Expenses (incl. Cost of Sales) are debits (LH), incomes are credits (RH)

Like this	(Dr)	(Cr)
Sales		X
Cost of Sales	X	
All overheads	X	

3. For every debit, there is a credit (and vice versa)

4. Do it the same way every time – this is honoured more in the breach than the observance. Remember, this is a logic system, so don't change the logic.

How to work it out. You have made a transaction, and you know where it goes in your Profit & Loss Account or balance sheet, but you might worry about where the other entry might be:

Think of how cash moves – if this was a cash or bank transaction, e.g. you pay someone so cash goes out, then a reduction in the bank balance is a credit (reducing the bank asset). Where's the debit likely to be? And a hint – most double entries are Profit & Loss and balance sheet, or sometimes balance sheet and balance sheet but never Profit & Loss and Profit & Loss.

Here are some quick examples of common entries

	Dr	Cr
1. Sell on credit – credit Sales (Profit & Loss Account)		X
debit Debtors (Customer owes you – balance sheet)	X	
2. Pay supplier – credit Bank (balance sheet)		X
debit Supplier (reduce Creditors – balance sheet)	X	
3. Pay salary or expense – debit Profit & Loss Account	X	
credit Bank (balance sheet)		X

4

Working Capital Cycle – This is Important

What is it?

Simply put, it's how money is used in the business. The money you get from sales is used to pay suppliers, which allows you to get more stock (on credit), pay the running costs of the business, and hopefully yourself. If the business is growing there is a need to make sure that you collect enough to fund the extra stock you will need for more sales and subsequently bigger supplier payments.

Here is an example of how double-entry helps us understand how working capital works.

You sell an item: Sell for cash (bank), sales (credit) go up, and bank balance increases (debit)

You sell on credit, so customers pay you later: Sales go up (credit) – where is the debit? It's Debtors – your customer owes you money, which is an asset. Then you get paid, turning one asset (credit entry to debtor) into another (debit entry to bank).

You pay your supplier, so you reduce your liability (debit to the supplier) by reducing your asset (credit to the bank).

So far so good. Keep the balance between debtors, cash and creditors (plus taxes etc.) and all is well. Get a lot more sales from customers/debtors (who pay later) – will you have enough cash to pay creditors on time? Managing debtor and creditor balances is key to staying in business.

Why it is Vital

You always have to balance the need to sell more and so earn more with the need to be able to pay people on time.

Businesses fail when they run out of cash, not because they are unprofitable.

It's quite easy to make a lot of sales and profits and still fail. The faster you grow, the greater the risk. It's called **overtrading**. Tuning Working Capital is key to survival. Grow carefully.

The Entrepreneur's Dilemma – Overtrading

Overtrading occurs in a period of very rapid growth. That's very common in the early days of a new business. What happens is that the costs necessary to support the business running at the level you expect it to be are too small to support it at the level that it actually is right now. You've planned for a larger turnover, and you've had to invest to achieve that.

If you're investing using future receipts – perhaps customers are paying you in advance before you do the work – then if they decide they don't want the work done, they will want their money back, and you are instantly unable to trade. As it is, if you make a loss, you may well become insolvent, and the law forbids you from trading. That's easy enough to avoid in the early days if you are investing for future growth. You can continue if you have firm plans that will not allow that loss to increase and, over time, reduce as the business grows.

To achieve that, you may have to cut down the rate of growth so that instead of having a fast, steep growth line, you slow it down so that the curve flattens out for a bit and the sales match the costs and you can recoup some of your cash. Then you can grow again.

Remember, growth usually involves bleeding cash for the growing element until it catches up (you may have to pay suppliers or new employees before sales happen and customers pay). That cash bleed is a loss that can only be funded by existing work or by cash put into the business. Too fast growth can exhaust the cash, and you can crash and burn from too much success.

You also have to be sure that your cost base and your business model work at different levels of activity. Entrepreneurs are naturally optimistic. That's a good thing, but over-optimism causes as many problems as it solves. Your plans must be based on reasonable assumptions and not just hope. Your business model has to be capable of being scaled, so you mustn't assume that the same model will work at different levels of activity. Usually, it won't. You must go back and check regularly. If you are trading whilst insolvent, you must document that you've done this; otherwise, it is likely that the directors of the business will be personally liable for any debts if the business goes down. If they've made reasonable assumptions and acted on them, mixed with a good dose of reality in that they have management accounts to check whether that is working or not, then they should be okay. It's very helpful to discuss this with your accountant, too, as that also gives you some protection from being pursued by your creditors. Taking professional advice is some defence – as long as you take it.

What you take out of the business must also be reasonable with what it earns. Business owners should get the largest slice of the pie. They put in all the risk and most of the effort, so this should be rewarded accordingly. Whilst it might be the largest slice, it's definitely the last one. It's after everybody else has been paid. If they have expectations and lifestyles, that means their slice of the pie doesn't fit the size of business that they have at the moment, then they need to scale that down. Creditors will not be sympathetic if they have lost money because the directors have taken too much out to fund the lifestyle that they think they deserve.

So, what's to be done? Regular, accurate, on-time management information is a must for any fast-growing business. Check your plans against that information and test to see what happens if turnover goes up a lot or drops significantly. What can you do to cut your cost base or to increase capacity with sufficient headroom to earn a profit and pay back any likely losses? As long as you can demonstrate this, you should be okay with your creditors, and it is more likely that you will be able to trade successfully. It's not just about covering your back; the same principles work in actually making the business successful.

Case Study on how to Restrict Growth

A security company was doing well and growing. So, the owner decided he deserved a reward and leased a nice Jaguar. Next year, there was downturn, caused by the loss of key employees, so the company couldn't fulfil all its contracts. But the lease of the Jaguar still had to be paid. The owner justified keeping it as he argued that customers expected to see a successful firm. But the cash outflow meant that the business had to manage cash very carefully and could not invest for the future. The Jaguar, by the way, was only one symptom of his strange thought process.

You Come Last – Sorry!

As a business owner, it means you don't get to spend the extra profits you are making from your growing business until the rate of increase in sales slows down, as you will always need more cash to fuel the Working Capital cycle. It can seem like you are working harder for nothing, but that's not true – your accounts will show you that you are doing better, and you should be able to make a guess when you can increase the money from the business to reward yourself. You will need to manage your own expectations.

If you can, do try to manage your growth so that you have a period of growth followed by a period of consolidation. That's when the cash catches up, and you can either pay yourself more or keep the cash to fuel the next growth phase.

What should happen is that you, the owner, should get the biggest slice of the cake. But remember, it's always the last slice of cake. Making sure you get the biggest slice needs constant attention, just as making sure you regularly get enough to eat.

What if we don't sell "stuff"?

This is still relevant if you have no stock, or what you sell is your time, or the time of your people in one form or another. Here, instead of stock and suppliers, you have the capacity (stock) of time and resources that you need to balance against the changing needs of customers.

Estate agents have no stock or saleable time, but they have properties for sale. They need to increase the stock of these to generate enough interest to sell them, and that takes time and money. And there's the time that the estate agent has to spend in selling the house and making sure the sale goes through. It's still a matter of capacity, just like physical stock.

So, every business will have something that primes the pump that generates sales. You will know what this is in your business.

A service business, selling time and resources, has more difficulty in adapting to changing demand than a business which sells things. This is because, with a business that sells things, the physical stock tap can be turned on and off much quicker. The service business may have to take on more people in the hope that their time can be sold quickly enough to at least make up for the extra cost. They've taken on a **fixed cost**. It may be better to subcontract until demand has built up to avoid having the difficulty of never filling the new capacity and having to lay someone off. Flexing stock levels to match demand is much quicker and cheaper, and it's always a variable cost.

Tuning Working Capital

There are only a few ways of managing **working capital**, but it does need constant attention, or else something will slip. Your cash flow will be impacted. So will your peace of mind.

Credit Terms

Get better credit terms from your suppliers – pay them slower. This frees up a one-off benefit to fuel more growth. One-off because if you suddenly get 60 days' credit on an extra £10k instead of 30 days, you have another £10k for a month but no more than that.

Get customers to pay quicker. Again, it fuels growth and it's a one-off. It also cuts your risk of a customer leaving you with a bad debt.

Ask for Discounts

If you're in the lucky position of having a healthy bank balance, ask your suppliers for a discount to pay them early. Another 5% off your direct costs, straight to bottom line profits, is a big benefit. If your Cost of Sales is 50% and you can get 5% off, that's 2.5% extra profit. Whilst it doesn't sound like a lot, think of what you have to pay for it. That extra 2.5% could double your fun money – what you get to enjoy rather than just pay the household bills. Also, have a look at the **14 ways to charge more** if you want to get a bit more creative.

Turn the Wheel Faster to Scale Your Business

Turn the Working Capital wheel faster – manage stock or people such that you utilise those assets quicker – it's about stock turn (how quickly you sell your stock, or your time) and how often, so that means minimum stock for maximum turn. Coupled with good credit terms and quick customer payments terms, this spins the wheel faster, so you get more profitable sales paying you quicker from the same amount of Working Capital. This is the key to continual improvement.

It's all in **5 steps to scaling your business**. Whether you want to scale or not, these steps make your business easier to control, more profitable and more predictable. And you can turn that Working Capital wheel faster. It's the equivalent of gears on a bike. Do you want a bike where you have to pedal more to go faster? Or would gears help?

5 Steps to Scaling Your Business

If you want to effect a business transformation and scale it significantly, certain things have to be done almost before you break ground.

Work out the **workflows**

Work out the **procedures** to ensure that the workflows happen

Organise **training** so that people follow the procedures

Design a **monitoring** system

Set up your **accounting** system

Only then can you be sure that your objectives might be achieved in a reasonably consistent manner. If you don't do these things first, it's likely that your monitoring will be slow and late and will be some sort of guesswork because you won't know which bit of your system is creaking and how it affects the others.

If you don't act at the beginning, you will end up putting out a lot of small fires instead of steering the ship.

Your decisions will be based on more guesswork than you will be comfortable with, and it will all feel like hard work, and you won't achieve everything that you're aiming for.

The danger of linear thinking

It's important to recognise that the route to growth is far from linear and if we wait for one thing to be done before we start the next it's very likely that your growth will be slower and more difficult.

Unfortunately, we tend to assume most things are linear when a moment's thought proves to us that almost everything isn't. Apart from the misdirection it gives, linear thinking utterly confounds any sort of planning. A linear plan means that because A happened, then we can now do B. If A doesn't happen, then everything following it doesn't happen, not just B but all the C, D, etc. actions that follow. Sometimes, we can make A happen, but with more effort, cost and time. And A may still make B fail because B was time-limited, or you don't have the resources any more, or for some other reason. Changing thinking sounds hard, but it does not need to be if you break it down into easy chunks.

Workflows that work for you

Why work out workflows? After all, you know how your business works, don't you? No one else in your team does. Also, you have enough experience to be able to improvise when things don't quite go to plan. No one else can do that.

If you start with the attitude that no one can do it better than you, you will be busy (very busy), but you won't grow.

Growth means getting other people to do the work. Which means telling and showing them how. Which means writing it down. If you don't, you will tell one person one thing and another person a slightly different version. Neither of them will remember it all, they will talk amongst themselves, and you will get version 3. Growth means some standardisation of approach. It doesn't mean standardisation of customer experience. You can still personalise what customers get, but your approach will be very similar each time.

It is easiest to draw your workflows rather than write each detailed procedure at a time. Make sure you add in the interfaces between people and departments, so, for example, how will someone know when to send an invoice on completion of a sale? Include a method of feeding back to you (or your supervisor/managers, etc.) when it doesn't go according to plan. Build in IFTTT (if this, then that) loops so your people know what to do in most situations when it goes a little off-road. Online tools to show this are available quite cheaply.

Workflows are not just for the technical parts of the job. They can be used to include how you get new customers, onboard them, and then do the work – create the app, build the house, etc., get the customer to agree it's done, invoice them, and collect payment. Your team will see how each part they are responsible for relates and depends on other parts, so improving understanding, and saving effort.

Procedures come next

Now, you can get into the details of the procedures for each element of the workflow. This needs to be written down – bullet points with examples of forms and checklists, etc, will do. Checklists? They produce a standard result, saving time on rework and avoiding mistakes. Next, walk through it – does it actually work that way? What needs to happen to information so that it gets from one procedure to the next? Once they are all done, ask someone else to see if they can follow it – your vocabulary will be a little different, as will your experience.

Without a doubt, you will have unrecorded knowledge that needs to be included to complete the procedure.

Training

Does this sound like a lot of work? It can be, but as you are running a business you want to grow, you need to act like a business owner, not a one-man band and try to go it alone. Doing it once means that every time you take on someone new, you don't have to repeat yourself or fight every day because they don't understand something. There are workflows and procedures for them to follow, which speed up their training and make them effective team members quicker.

As you did for procedures, write out what you want people to learn and how you want them to learn it. On the job, classroom, short chat, video (video the short chat). Script the important bits so that everyone gets the same message every time you deliver it.

Monitoring system

This isn't just the accounts. The books record the past and, as such, have limited use in helping your decision-making. You need metrics from the number of sales enquiries, how many you convert, average order value, how many you can complete and invoice in a given time, how productive your people are and so on. Your business will have some industry-standard measures and your own unique ones. How will you know, and how quickly do you need to know? A lot of it can be automated, even in some trades, so there's no reason why you can't get this promptly and accurately. And you get to feed in your procedures and ways of populating your monitoring systems.

Here are some workflows that might apply to a builder:

Marketing

Onboarding a customer

Quoting, including bill of materials

Scheduling and allocating people and goods

Getting materials on time on site and in the right quantity, receiving supplier invoices and paying them

Monitoring the work

Dealing with delays, shortages, and work order changes

Completion and sign-off

Invoicing and cash collection

Procedures can be developed for all of these, and monitoring would be against project timelines, actual cost against budget, cash flow and overall profitability. These can be fed back during the job to ensure it finishes on time and on budget or that variances are known early and managed to minimise losses. Information from this job informs the next one.

Accounting system

This is last because it records earlier decisions. Your accounts system should be able to draw from other systems to make life as integrated as possible, so you get the information you need on time, accurately and easily. For example, once your job scheduling system gets to the client acceptance stage, it then takes the quote and turns it into an invoice. Apart from saving you time, the accuracy and speed of recording enables you to make better decisions quicker.

Value your time

Systemising takes you away from doing the work to managing the work and thinking about how the business can thrive. This is, after all, your job alone. So many times, I have seen growth stalled because the owner does too much that could be outsourced, automated or offloaded to someone else. No thinking time equals no growth. No busy fools here please.

No thinking time = no growth

See the value of your time below.

5

Key Data

Functional relationships

Look at these in detail frequently (weekly or daily), and ensure you know the relationships between/among them

1. Sales and the cost of selling
2. Gross Profit
3. Direct costs – what are they in your business? Examples might be salaries
4. Working Capital
5. Bank balance
6. Aged debtors/receivables (who owes you for how long)
7. Aged creditors/payables (who you owe for how long)
8. Don't forget you may have to pay VAT and payroll taxes regularly, so build that into your cash planning

What other key relationships are there? They are not all in the bookkeeping detail. How about the number of leads, number converted, cost of a lead, etc? How will you capture and measure this data? If you've done **business plans and forecasts**, these assumptions will be written down there, so it's very helpful to check them, as they show how you think your business works versus how it actually works. The actual numbers tell you if you are right and hint at what to do about it if you aren't.

Look at Monthly or Quarterly

If they are significant, look at your most variable overheads. What is significant? You should be able to spot them easily enough. Don't get into too much detail – pick out the main 3 at most you need to concentrate on and do what you can to change them. Anything that might be a fixed cost (maybe you paid the rent that month so that figure stands out), you can usually ignore, unless there is a trend.

Look at annually or when you change them (a new hire, for example)

Fixed costs – can you turn any into variable costs? Why would you want to? Because an extra fixed cost, such as an admin salary, means you will have to make so many more sales at your gross profit % just to stay still. Some of that extra cost, if you are growing, will be wasted until you have grown, for example, when that admin person is busy all day.

Example

> Admin costs £12000 a year, Gross Profit is 30%.
>
> To get an extra £12000 at Gross Profit at 30% you have to sell an extra £40000 of product. (12000/0.30)

Outsourcing turns this into a variable cost for whatever hours you need, until you are spending £12000, when you might bring it back in-house. You might want to think about outsourcing whatever fixed cost that you can. Turning fixed into variable costs also makes them easier to manage and relieves pressure on you to make more sales.

The Value of Your Time

Let's assume you value your time at £50 an hour. If a job makes you or saves you £50 or more in an hour, then do it yourself. If less, then get one of your team to do it or outsource it.

Doing your own admin stops you from doing work that brings in money or thinking about how to make your business better. It doesn't matter what hourly rate an outsource firm charges; it matters how long they take, so what really matters is the value they give you.

If they specialise in the work that you need to do perhaps – to get it done, they will be quicker and better than you. If they can do it for less than £50 an hour or in fewer hours than you, then give it to them.

Illustration

Bookkeeping takes you 2 hours a week at £50 = £100

Qualified bookkeeping firm takes 1 hour at £60. And they are likely to do it a lot better than you. Give it to them.

Most SMEs should outsource their bookkeeping, turning it into a variable cost and getting better information to make better decisions.

Read then Safely Ignore

These are terms for you to understand and for your accountant to handle. However, you should tell your accountant before you make any decisions that might change these elements to avoid poor outcomes from extra costs or impacts on cash flow.

Depreciation. This is a non-cash accounting term designed, in its simplest form, to crudely measure the economic value that your fixed assets have produced over time, and to reduce your profits (but not your cash). This provides a mechanism so that you can replace the asset when it is worn out, from the cash which has been retained. The double-entry might help to explain it.

Depreciation is a debit, an expense in Profit & Loss Account and Credit against Fixed Assets in the balance sheet, so reducing year by year the profits available for drawings and the value of the assets. Whilst the lower profit means there is less for you to take as drawings, the cash hasn't been affected, so over time, the logic is that cash builds up, and so can be used to buy the new asset.

Profit/loss on sale. This is the accounting which happens very occasionally when you sell or scrap a fixed asset. It's the difference between the reduced asset figure after depreciation in the balance sheet and what you sold it for. Don't attempt to do it yourself – ask your accountant to make the entries. *Do tell your accountant as soon as you are thinking of buying or selling an asset as there may be tax implications.* Don't wait until after the event.

Interest. This is normally bank interest, overdraft or loan. Any loan payments you make are usually a mixture of interest and repayment of the amount loaned. So, it needs to be split so that the interest appears as an expense and the loan on the balance sheet gets reduced. Ask your accountant to set it up for you. Most online bookkeeping software allows this to happen the same way every time, so you will only need to ask once.

6

Variances and Trends

How to Compare one Set of Figures with Another

Remember, this is all past performance and needs balancing with relevance to future plans. So, by all means, use it to reduce costs where you sensibly can and to make changes, but also feed back into your **Business plans and forecasts**. All this adds considerably to your understanding of how the business ought to work, how it is working and what you can do about it.

Most digital bookkeeping packages list overheads alphabetically, which isn't particularly helpful. You can group them in the chart of accounts either by logical elements like Marketing and sales, Finance, Establishment (premises) costs, etc, or you can group them by fixed and variable. Both work and some packages allow you to do both, so you could, for example, group by logical elements and then sub-group by fixed and variable. The idea is to make them easier to read and understand so that your eye will naturally fall on the things which demand your attention. And you don't have to wade through lots of unnecessary listings, which wastes time.

Here's an example of how that can look.

Variance analysis

	This year to date	Last year to date	% Difference
Sales			
A	100000	90000	11.1
B	50000	60000	-16.7
C	120000	100000	20
Total sales	200000	220000	10
Cost of Sales			
Costs	189000	179000	5.6
Gross Profit	81000	71000	14.1
GP%	30%	28.4%	
Overheads			
Premises			
Fixed: Rent & rates	1000	1000	0
Fixed: Insurance	500	450	11.1
Fixed: Utilities	800	700	14.3
Repairs	900	200	450
Marketing & sales			
Fixed: Salaries	30000	27000	10
Fixed: Motor	5000	4000	25
Fixed: Phone & internet	1000	800	25
Variable: Commissions	8100	7100	14.1

Variable: Adverts	2500	2000	25
Finance			
Fixed: Bank charges	500	480	4.2
Fixed: Accountancy	2500	2200	13.6

Variances compare one period with another (similar) period or against budget/plan. Which ones should you look at? Before you dive into numbers, consider the context. You know what's going on in your business and the wider world, so the numbers need to be considered with that in mind. So, ask yourself, does this number generally make sense? Is it what you would expect?

If so, look at the numbers which relate to that. In this example, if sales have gone up from £200,000 to £220,000, would you expect sales commissions to go up by 10%? If yes, you don't need to look any more at commissions. But commissions have gone up by 14.1%. Why?

You might also be very interested in why sales of B have gone down whilst sales of C have gone up. You should also look at why the GP% has gone up. It might be that you have sold some old stock that was in the balance sheet, so there are no costs associated with it, or maybe you've put prices up. Whatever it is, you can see that the 1.6% rise in GP has brought you another £3520 in profit (sales of £220,000 x 1.6%). Has that gone straight down to the bottom line? If not, what has changed in the overheads, and which ones can you influence?

It would be pointless to try to list all the possible reasons figures can change. ***Remember the principle that for every change there is a change somewhere else – the double-entry***

effect. Finding the other entry might give you another insight. Then it's a question of putting it into context, and asking lots of questions, mainly why, or reflect on **Kipling's I Keep Six Honest Serving Men** until you are comfortable that you either need to act, or you don't.

Have a go and ask your accountant for help in interpreting the figures if you are unsure. You will learn and do better next time.

Other Comparisons you can Make

You can also compare plans, forecasts or budgets to discover the **relationships and assumptions** that aren't working and extrapolate. What will it mean to profits and cash flow if this continued? Do I need to change anything, or is it too small to worry about, or maybe it is a fixed cost so I can't do much about it anyway?

Trends look at variances over a longer time, so expand the variance analysis period. It enables you to see how a small variance month by month adds up and so might demand attention.

When looking at variances, try not to get too excited by the overheads. Most of them are fixed or may not vary too much. You can certainly look critically at them from time to time but don't spend too much effort on it. It's easy to try and trim costs, but not at the expense of the proper functioning of the business. It's also easier to look at these areas as they are under your control, whereas the sales and other, more important relationships involve external actors – customers and suppliers, not under your control. But it's here that most of the benefits accrue to you in analysing and understanding how the model in your head (or hopefully in your plan) of how the business should work contrasts with what is actually happening.

What Should you Concentrate on?

Actual sales vs. last period/budget and gross profit vs. last period/budget

I'm a fan of Year to Date (YTD) reports, especially This Year to Last Month vs. Last Year to Last Month and Actual/ Last YTD budget as well. I like to see what seasonality there is and how that compares with the last.

You can get into more detail – This week vs. Last week etc, but that is only really useful if you are tracking sales so that you can make a big push to get to the end of month budget. It works well if you catch any slippage early in the month, so you have time to catch up, rather than wait until after the month end when you can only measure what you have failed to do.

The simple way to do this is with a wall chart with the weekly sales budget and plot what you did week by week. Don't wait for the bookkeeping to catch up.

Remember, bookkeeping measures the past (even if it's the recent past), and you want to influence the present and the future.

7

Business Plans, Forecasts and Budgets

A plan and a forecast are very similar, and the terms are often used interchangeably. The difference is that a forecast is a prediction of future events, whereas a plan is how you intend to respond to that prediction. Hence, I think I will sell 100 of item A every week for £10 each is a forecast. Put this assumption (100 units at £10 each) into your plan of how you will make those sales.

A business plan is a model of what you think might happen, given certain assumptions.

Everyone has a plan, written down or not. Business owners build their business on the back of what they think will happen. But it doesn't ever happen quite like that.

I don't like the way business plans are used. It's usually just to get bank funding and then forgotten, except by the bank manager, who may well ask you why the plan isn't working. If the answer isn't good, the assumption is that you don't know how your business works and funding becomes difficult, or the bank withdraws it. Don't blame the bank. It's a reasonable point of view. If you can't explain it, you don't know! Would you lend money to someone who doesn't know how their business works?

Business owners don't like business plans as the reality turns out differently, so usually they are ignored. But that is a mistake – they have value. You need to understand what they are and, more importantly, what they are not. A business plan is not about what is going to happen. It is a model with assumptions. As reality intrudes, you can see which assumptions were wrong and by how much. And you can tweak your plan to predict what cash needs you will have before you run out of money, and how your profit changes, or what you might be able to do about sales prices or some costs. Time spent on tuning how the business works reaps dividends.

All plans make assumptions – be explicit in your plan and write down how you think the business works, e.g. I will sell 100 of item A every week for £10 each. Every week, including Christmas? Discovering which assumptions are wrong is very helpful. It allows for re-jigging the plan and informs how relationships change and how working capital needs to change. It's a good idea to tell the bank when things are going wrong and how you are going to fix them before the bank calls you. Give the bank confidence that you know how to run your business.

Banks understand that things change; it's how you react and how fast you react that is important.

And it may be that things are going better than planned, and you need more funding. Best to ask early and not risk having to turn sales away because you might run out of cash (see **Working Capital Cycle**). Also, this allows you to test new ideas in the planning model without betting everything on the house.

A budget is a more micro-level look at the coming year. So, you will look at your plan and break it down to exactly how much you will earn and spend on each bookkeeping line. And then you can see, as time passes, what works and what doesn't. The information you get can be fed back into the plan to see if you will get issues with cash or debt (or profits) further down the line. You will get the information to see what is working through a **variance and trends** analysis.

It sounds like a lot of work, but it needn't be. Run all 3 documents concurrently so one feeds into the other, forecasts into the plan, and the plan into the budget. There will be time to make sales and run the business, never fear.

Rolling budgets

These are usually a rolling 12 months, so that you never end a budget period. The benefit is that you always have a future view of your business and how it works, but the downside is that you may not pause and re-evaluate the business from first principles, which is easier with an annual budget. At some point, you need to critically examine each element and see if it is fit for purpose, be it your systems, workflows, products and services, etc. It's easier if you are using an annual budget.

Whichever you use, don't treat this as a mechanical exercise. It should help inform you which assumptions aren't working and will help you in pricing and capacity decisions, as well as what costs need attention. It's helpful to do 'What If' planning. Change volumes and prices of what you sell and what you buy to give you an idea of how sensitive the business is to change. For example, if your sales dropped by 10%, what would that do to profits? And what if your suppliers increased their prices by 5%? Or have customers started taking 60 days to pay instead of 30 days? When something outside of your control changes, as it inevitably will, you will have a much better idea of what changes you can make to cope.

How do I get paid?

Sales minus costs should create a profit and fund your dividends or drawings.

NB More dividends mean a lower bank balance and so more strain on Working Capital. Try to balance what you need now against what the business might need if it hits a problem, which at some point it will.

Remember you personally have fixed and variable costs too – too much in your fixed costs means it's difficult to change if there is a problem in the business. So, go easy on the big mortgage and car, and hire purchase – set yourself a % of what should be fixed costs. Give yourself some slack. You and the business are interchangeable to some extent. Yes, you have to make sure that the business and you operate as separate personalities from a legal perspective, but everyone recognises that you are running this business to fulfil personal goals. So, you should think of your personal costs in the same way as those of your business. Keep fixed costs as low as you can and have enough put by to weather any storm.

Number one personal wealth creating tip – pay down debt! Especially as debt is almost always a fixed cost. Here are some hints on what money might mean to you. Also, if you owe debt – be it a bank loan in the business, mortgage or personal loan – someone else has a say in how you run your business and your life.

What Money Might Mean to You?

If you invest in a fund and manage it yourself, will you make, over time, the same return as the fund manager does, a better return or a worse return? Usually, it's a worse return. Illogical until we bring in the human factor.

Behaviour not skill

Do you gamble? You know that gambling is a fool's game. Gamblers study the form – sports pages, they listen to pundits, and then they place a bet and watch for the result. It's fun! Costly fun, but still fun. It's predicated on the search for knowledge and then the need to take some action. Something gets you excited, and you do something.

Do you look at share prices? Do you look at share tips? And do you get excited and do something?

Black Monday. 9 October 1987, stock markets around the world crashed. More than 20% was wiped off share prices worldwide. Clients of mine had only a few weeks earlier invested in a range of investments after careful consideration of trading history, likely prospects, etc. They lost over £30,000 overnight. They panicked and sold, whereas laziness (inaction) would have saved all their losses, as 6 months later, their funds were trading back at pre-crash levels.

This is only one example of crashes and panics around the world. There were 10 documented in the 19th century, 15 in the 20th, and so far 11 this century, the last being caused by the EU Referendum result. Some were caused by automated trading systems (but programmed by people), and some were caused by old fashioned investor panic. All can be traced back to sentiment.

How can you stop yourself from being affected by sentiment?

What does money mean to you?

You need to ask yourself some fundamental questions before you can assess what you need to do and how you might go about it.

Ask yourself what personal objectives you are seeking to achieve in growing your wealth. Money is not an end in itself – it's what it allows you to do. What do you want it for?

You need to consider timeframes, what lifestyle you want for yourself and yours, what a secure retirement looks like, and how these objectives might change over time. These are just examples. You need to think about it from your perspective.

Then, and only then, it's time to ask yourself how you function and make sure you catch yourself before you do anything that is so much "fun" it costs you.

Three questions

Ask yourself 3 questions before you make any change:

If this goes well, what impact will it have?

If it goes badly, what impact will it have?

Have I been wrong before (be honest, it's yes!)?

This is about risk modelling

Risk modelling

Will the change have a big impact but a small risk? (Maybe do it)

Will it have a big impact, a big risk? (Mitigate it – not all eggs in one basket)

Will it have a small impact but a big risk? (Don't even think about it)

Then, do I have to take this risk? Usually, you don't have to. You want to – the fun aspect.

If I take this risk, can I eliminate the risk?

If I can't eliminate the risk, can I mitigate it? That is what a bookmaker does when laying off a large bet to other bookmakers.

Remember, risk is a function of probability and impact. High impact? Why do it?

Considerations like this allow you to diversify a portfolio, balance risk and rewards and ultimately, if you leave well alone, build wealth.

This applies just as well to major business issues as well as buying and selling shares. Make a decision, don't overthink, don't get excited and feel you have to act. Exercise self-control and self-confidence. Avoid thinking "I have to make a decision, this is a decision, therefore I will make it." Do you really have to, and even then is there an alternative? Be "ignorant and lazy." Then you will at least match the market, not lag it.

A guaranteed risk-free return? I've already told you. Pay down debt!

8

Cost Cutting

This is generally a knee-jerk reaction to a crisis. Don't. If you must, cut once and deep; don't fiddle and revisit. Do it once and get down to a minimum to run the business successfully. But don't negatively affect delivering the service. Before any cost measures, consider what is **fixed and what is variable,** as well as **the relationships between elements.**

Cost cutting is different from cost control. Cost control is a regular look at what is costing you money, what value you are receiving, and what you might do about it. Don't look at everything. Look at meaningful amounts. See **Variances and trends.**

Time Management

Your time is precious. Don't waste it on small items, when you could be looking at the bigger picture and, for example, influencing your customers and markets. Whilst you need to spend time on managing your numbers, these are largely internal actions. Make sure most of your focus is external, i.e. customers. Look again at **The value of your time.**

An easy way to ensure that your time on the numbers is well spent is to set up your accounts systems so the books are accurate, up-to-date, and easy to read so you can zoom in on the elements that need your attention. Talk to your accountant if you haven't got an online bookkeeping solution and get one set up. If you have this already, ask what reports you should be using and how to find them. Most software packages allow you to save report formats, so you can find them easily next time.

9

Sales Management

Sales management is about prioritising customers. Ask yourself who is most valuable to you, pays you best, pays on time and gives you the least amount of grief.

There is a useful rule called The Pareto Principle, where 80% of consequences come from 20% of causes. Using the same principle, you could say 20% of your customers probably give you 80% of sales, but what **markup v margin** are they producing? You can investigate that using Pareto as well. Using this approach helps you to recognise who is most valuable and needs most attention.

Remember, you can't eat sales; you eat profits. Look at your margins.

All Customers are not the Same

List your customers by type – not limited company, individual etc, but by value to you as small, medium, large (rank 1-5), what they buy from you, what they could be buying from you, how well they pay, what margin they produce, and maybe how easy they are to deal with.

A simple table will do, like this:

Customer name	S/M/L	Main purchases	Could be purchased	Payments (1-5)	Margin (1-5)	Easy to deal with (1-5)

Think about what would happen if you stopped dealing with the smaller customers who produce the worst margins and, almost certainly, give you the most hassle. Without even constructing the table, you know exactly who they are! Pareto rules apply here, too – almost certainly, 20% of your customers give you 80% of the problems.

How much time might the exercise shown in the table free up to spend with your best customers, who might buy more from you, given a little more attention? Should you give every customer the same level of care and attention?

Remember that every customer carries an admin and overhead load in your business. In other words, it takes time and money to service a customer – any customer, no matter how good or bad. You need to set them up on your systems, maintain the data, make the sales, invoice, collect the money, etc.

It's easy enough to look at the time and therefore cost to you per customer. Then look at what they bring you in margin and how much hassle they are to deal with. Finally, decide whether to keep or lose that customer. Yes, seriously! **And this is how**.

Ask yourself this question – if you got rid of a lot of your smaller customers, does that free up time which you could better direct towards getting more sales from the better customers? Or can you cut the admin overhead? Or, better still, spend more time on marketing to get better customers? Now is a good time to see if dropping some customers allows you to drop some costs, too. More net profit for less effort? It has been done and is done by all the best-performing businesses. Don't you deserve better?

All You offer is not the Same Value

List your services – who isn't buying some of them? Why not? What can be done about that? What margins does each product or service produce for you?

Could you offer discounts if a customer bought more of something, or a bundle of 2 or more things? That might be cost effective if you make one delivery instead of two. Or for paying quicker?

Or could you unbundle some of your offerings and sell them individually and make more money? Do you do special offers, such as Christmas, Easter, Valentine's Day, Holi, Ramadan etc? Is there any seasonal activity in your business, so that a special offer in the quieter months might help boost sales and cash flow? Or perhaps you may decide to make a special offer, just because, and see if it works for you.

Business is a series of small experiments. Double down on the ones that work and stop the ones that don't – fast.

Setting Prices

Can you increase your prices even a little? Most small business owners are very reluctant to increase prices as it might scare a customer away, but they haven't worked out what it could mean if they did.

Example

> You make 30% gross profit, so every £100 gets you £30.
>
> If you put your prices up by 10% across the board (you might cherry pick products and services), how many customers (and sales) would you have to lose to be in the same position?
>
> Sales are now £110 and gross profit is £40.
>
> The answer is 17% of your customers by value, on average.

Is that likely? If so, which ones do you think would leave?

Would you care if all of them or just some left, and which ones? It is more likely that the smallest, worst paying, more time-consuming customers would leave, who you might be glad to see the back of anyway (see, **All customers are not the same**). If you annoyed someone you wanted to keep, you can always backtrack. Or you might only increase prices for the small annoying customers, so turning them into better customers, should they decide to stay and pay more. It's worth thinking about how your customers behave towards you. Here are some thoughts on whether you have transactions with customers or build relationships and how you can **manage your customers better**.

Absolute or relative problems

Most issues we have ever faced are relative. A dip in some areas, which affect us, but not all at once. If we are in an absolute phase, then everyone is affected to some extent or other. Activity levels have dropped, not just in your sector.

When we deal with relative issues, it is up to us to manage to claw our way back to what was parity. Others are still carrying on as though nothing had happened.

Our response to an absolute dip is to maintain what we can at lower levels. By that, we mean finding ways to keep everything going in our value chain. We need our customers, suppliers, team and other stakeholders to still be there, albeit at this new lower activity level. We need to keep everything going. The essence of it is that we are all in it together.

When the world starts to change again, it won't all change back at the same rate or at the same time. There will be false dawns, faster progress in some areas and little or no change in others. Winners and losers will start to emerge. We won't all be in it together – we will have changed into a relative environment. It will get competitive.

Transactions or relationships

We want our value chains to be about relationships. That binds us all together better and produces better results for us. Firstly, amongst our customers, but also our suppliers and team.

You will have transactional encounters with customers in some cases. This is where it's all about price, quantity and delivery. There is little opportunity to build a relationship or add any more value. You can probably already identify the transactional people you deal with now.

Being transactional is the default position for many businesses in a crisis.

What you can do to shield yourself

After any major change, there will be winners and losers. Plan now which one you want to be.

Defensive tactics

Start with 3 lots of triage for your customers and suppliers.

1. Divide customers into – Can't Pay or Won't Pay.

2. Designate customers and suppliers T (Transactional) or R (Relationship).

3. Designate customers 1-5 for the risk of their business failure.

Your 1-5 risk ranking will allow you to allocate resources where it will do the most good. This is by supporting customers and suppliers who you think will last the course. Not all will be R's, though, so make sure that, with each of them, you play by their rules to your advantage. Remember that a number of small businesses fail, and no doubt some large ones. Expect to lose customers and suppliers.

Expect a lot of your T's to shop around more. Be prepared to trim prices or lose customers. If some are high risk, you may want to let them leave anyway. You don't want them failing when they are a customer of yours, owing you money.

You may well find that Won't Pay customers are T's. Don't waste time appealing to their better natures. If they can afford to pay you but won't, sue them. If they insist on using their own rules, play by those rules to your advantage or you will lose out. They won't take it personally. Neither should you.

Assume the worst, and plan for the best. So, go through the skill sets and capacity in the team you currently have. Are there overlaps or gaps that you can cut if there is a drop in activity? Can you turn a fixed cost like a salary into a variable cost by outsourcing some work? Do you provide a service which you can offer as a variable cost to potential customers?

Support your community whatever it looks like – be that where you live and work or your business community. If you can make an offer that helps your value chain or a wider one, make that offer if there's little or no cost to you.

Do all you can to support your customers – but not the ones you think might fail, or the Ts. They won't appreciate it. Make sure your community knows about it – you want them to call you first when their life gets back to some sort of normality.

Offensive tactics

Triage your competitors. For those you think might be at risk, try to ensure that when they fail, their customers come to you. They will be more receptive to offers. Once they have experienced and trusted you, you can develop relationships. Businesses that survive will have more available market share.

Some of your current team may be transactional, i.e. not engaged with your business. It's a chance to upskill your team by getting them engaged, or changing them. Team engagement is a whole new topic, outside the scope of this book.

Leadership shifts

You may wince at the directness of some of this – it isn't how you want to be, and it may not sit well with your values. I agree. It's not me either. Leadership can't ever afford rose tinted spectacles and action is better than feeling helpless. You won't be able to live by your values if your business has ceased.

You don't need to be aggressive, but you can be firm, and you need to be attuned to subtle changes in the behaviour of your customers and suppliers so you can protect your business and your team. Economic downturns happened in 2008, 1999, and 1987. There will be others. It's about staying in the game, and if these are the rules, you have to follow them. Later, you can change back. That's not to say you have to change completely. Be your true self. Help where you can, be kind and supportive where it's appreciated.

If you do nothing and hope for the best, you may well survive, but certainly you'll be weaker. Or you can come out of this stronger. It's up to you. Don't feel helpless – take action.

The point is that the choice is yours. Don't make a decision through inaction. Regularly review your prices, and don't be afraid of small increases. Here are a couple of very small changes and what they can mean to you.

Example

Let's say your Profit & Loss account looks like this:

Sales		1000
Cost of Sales		500
Gross Profit		500
Overheads		400
Net Profit	10%	100

You increase the sales price by 1%.

Sales		1010
Cost of Sales		500
Gross Profit		510
Overheads		400
Net Profit	10% up from 100	110

Or decreasing Cost of Sales by 2% gives exactly the same result. That could be better prices from suppliers or doing the work faster, or a bit of both. An increase in sales price of 1% and a decrease in Cost of Sales of 2% increases your net profit, not by 10% but 20%!

Sales		1010
Cost of Sales		490
Gross Profit		520
Overheads		400
Net Profit	20% up from 100	120

In the example above, you made £100 net profit. This funds your lifestyle, paying for mortgage or rent, food, utility bills, tax, etc. and leaves, we hope, some money over for enjoyment. Your fun money can easily be no more than 10% of your £100. How much more enjoyment can be had if £10 could be turned into £30 by adding that extra £20 to your bottom line with those 2 simple changes?

Markup vs Margin – Know the Difference

Muddling markup and margin leads to business failure, as does reliance on percentages without any appreciation of the raw numbers. I will show you an example with real consequences later. And a few tips on how to price for profit.

To remind you, let's get some quick definitions out of the way.

Cost of Sales means things that you buy to sell. That could be simply something you buy and then resell, or it could be components that you put together to sell such as parts in a computer, or it could be your team's time that you sell.

Direct costs are expenses you incur in achieving the sale. The obvious one is carriage. All costs other than direct costs are overheads.

Your margin is the difference between the Cost of Sales and the sales for a particular item.

The gross profit percentage is the margin divided by sales.

Markup vs Margin

Often people talk about markup. That means cost plus a profit figure to arrive at sales price. The difficulty arises when they muddle both terms.

Here's a simple example. Let's say the sales price is £7.50, and Cost of Sales is £5.

The markup from £5 to £7.50 is £2.50 (50%). But it's only 33.3% gross profit. That's £2.50 / £7.50.

It's quite common to see people work only in percentages and end up making a loss this way.

Case Study

I used to have a client who sold computers and made this exact mistake. He thought, using those figures, that he was making a 50% margin and constructed his business to fit with that assumption (see below), with reality in the second column:

	Assumption	**Reality**
Sales	100%	100%
Cost of Sales	50%	66%
Gross profit (margin) %	50%	33%
Premises costs	10%	10%
Team costs	20%	20%
Other costs	10%	10%
Profit/loss	10%	- 7%

He never believed the accounts we produced, even when we reconciled them to his books and showed him what his mistake was. He couldn't, or wouldn't see it, as he couldn't bring himself to believe he could sell at 100% markup which would give the business a 50% margin. He persisted with his assumption, and sadly the company, and he, went bankrupt.

How to Game Yourself With Numbers

Once upon a time, there was a very small Taiwanese company called Asus – now the third-largest computer company in the world. It just made DRAM chips, which go into microprocessors.

They went to Dell, who made and controlled everything in the production of their computers, and said "we can make DRAM chips 20% cheaper than you can and this is our business, we're really good at it, why don't we do this for you and you stop making DRAM chips?"

Dell agreed as they were 20% cheaper so Dell's margins got better, and they didn't have to stock all these DRAM chips so they needed less cash.

Time passed, and Asus went back to Dell and said, "We make microprocessors now, and we do it really well; we can make them 20% cheaper than you can, so why don't we do that for you?" Dell looked at the microprocessors and said yes, Asus can make them 20% cheaper, and if we buy from Asus, we don't have to worry about yet more stock, so we will do it. And so, Dell's margins went up again, and Asus became more profitable, and they were both happy.

A pattern emerges, the essence being that Asus kept going back to Dell and kept saying we can do this part of your business 20% cheaper than you can, and we're really good at it, so why can't we do it? And Dell, every time, said yes, they can do it 20% cheaper, and they are good at it, and we can stop all these supply chain issues and all the management of that, we can stop all this capital expenditure, we can get really lean and have really high margins, and they did that until... Asus produced the whole computer, and all Dell did was market it.

Asus had squeezed Dell out of the whole business because Dell has chased margin and not net profit. Because they only looked at the margin, which is a ratio (percentage) they lost the plot a little bit about what their core business really was and how they could protect it. And now you see Asus branded computers all over the place – they're really good – just as good as Dell!

Dell noticed – eventually – which is why you can buy Asus and Dell kits now.

Gross margin is really important. But it's not the whole thing. Large businesses are very good at measuring the wrong things sometimes. Whereas a small business sees the thing it is producing or the service it's giving as discrete units, which gives it an advantage, as it's not got a management team whose goals are completely obsessed by the margins.

Remember, though, that all businesses are at the mercy of competitive pressures or sometimes people being "helpful" like Asus. We are very much in favour of strategic partnerships, but that doesn't necessarily mean giving the family silver away piece by piece. If Dell had concentrated on net profit, which other companies have done in the face of similar pressures, they would have noticed sooner. And every time, it was a good management decision that eroded their market! Managers were being measured on the wrong things internally, and so looking at the wrong measures and failing to see the units.

The other point is simply this – Dell gamed themselves by following their own self-imposed rules. No one forced them to adopt them. Which ones are you gaming yourself with?

Get back to the real numbers. And, of course, if you need to price for profit, make sure you don't muddle markup with margin. And listen to your accountant!

Pricing and Contribution

You can't always get what you want. You may want a 50% gross profit (there's a table of common markup and related margins further down for reference), but you can't always get it. How can you work out whether it's worthwhile taking something at a lower margin? Here's how to work out a decent price that still makes you money. A reminder of 2 definitions.

Fixed and Variable Costs– Know the Difference

Fixed costs do not change with activity levels. The obvious fixed cost is rent. Until you get so busy you must go to bigger premises, the rent is fixed. It is something you must pay every month or quarter and you must have enough sales at enough margin to pay it. Most other premises costs are pretty much fixed, such as the business rates, and light and heat. Often salaries are effectively fixed, month to month.

Variable costs vary with activity. So, for example, sales team commissions or motor expenses might vary with the level of sales.

Knowing the difference between fixed and variable costs is crucial to price-setting

Recognising which are the variable costs and how they move with the activity levels will tell you how much extra variable cost you're going to incur in selling one more thing. That eats into your margin but gives you a clearer idea of how you can price something and still make a profit. So, whilst you may not get your full margin, you're still making something which will soak up some of your fixed costs and contribute to profit.

Here's a simple example.

Sales	1000 @10	
		10000
Cost of Sales	1000 @5	
		5000
Margin (gross profit)	1000 @5	
		5000
Fixed costs		
		2000
Variable costs	1000 @1	
		1000
Profit		**2000**

Every unit sold costs £10, has sales costs of £5 and a variable cost of £1. This means that every unit has a **contribution** of £4 towards fixed overheads and profit. From that, it's easy to decide how much you can discount a unit and still make a worthwhile profit. You will have other decisions, such as whether the customer will want that discount every time or can you make it a one-off, whether you can squeeze more volume sales to justify the price cut, etc. There's one caveat. You can only consistently price this way if all your fixed costs are covered by existing sales. Otherwise, you may not have enough contribution to pay all your fixed costs.

Common markup and related margins

Mark up	Margin (gross profit %)
100%	50%
60%	37.5%
50%	33.3%
40%	28.5%
30%	23%
25%	20%

Anything smaller than 20% – ask yourself why you are selling it.

10

Do the Figures Make Sense?

Look first at the Profit & Loss Account – compare it with the last period, then last year, and then Year to Date/last Year to Date.

Is the shape of the reports similar? And if not, can you explain why?

What do I mean by shape?

It's the overall numbers – are they similar for each category, such as sales, Cost of Sales, and the various expense headings. Try looking at overall amounts first, and the proportions, then dig into detail on the parts that look odd. Don't dissect every figure. You need to take an overview and the shape will help you.

Is it what you expect? You will probably be quite obsessive about some elements. Sales per period and gross profit percentage, for certain. To help you, go to **Variances and trends** for an example. It needs a bit of practice, but over time, you will develop a feel for what looks right and what sticks out.

Now look at the balance sheet – again compare and look at the shape. Does this make sense, or have some numbers changed a lot?

For example, have your debtors gone down significantly? This could be because a lot of your customers have paid you recently, or it could be because you haven't sold very much. If it's the former, you should have more cash (remember the double-entry?) so you can pay suppliers and your working capital cycle isn't affected. But if it's the latter, then you might need to generate some sales and turn them into cash quickly so that you can keep trading, as suppliers will want to be paid.

Don't worry too much about the fixed assets and any long-term borrowings, as they don't change very much over time. Concentrate on the Working capital parts of the balance sheet.

Get Paid on Time

Invoice on time to get paid on time. Do not wait until the end of the month to do your invoices and then wonder why customers take yet another month to pay you. Consider this scenario because it happens:

You do the work month one 1 week 1

You send an invoice month 1 week 4

The invoice arrives at your customer at the very end of month 1

They decide to enter it in their books as day 1 and month 2 (I wonder why!)

They pay at the end of the month following **receipt** of invoice – that is now the end of month 3.

Can you afford that delay?

Often, a customer does only one payment run per month, so find out when and make sure your invoices arrive in time to be included. If you don't know how long it takes them to process an invoice (you probably don't), then ask them.

Send regular reminders, and, if possible, **Mechanise** this. Most cloud-based accounting software will send regular email reminders to your customers.

Case Study

A tree surgeon uses online bookkeeping, with an app on his phone. He's on time, very tidy, listens to his customers, and his prices are good. All told, he's excellent at his job. But he takes, on average, 2 months to follow up his quote with an invoice. He's owed thousands of pounds in unbilled work and complains he can't afford a new shredder as he hasn't any money. He could deliver the invoice via his app and get paid before he leaves the job. Newsflash – I have just paid his invoice for last year, as it was so late. Even then, I had to remind him 4 times.

Slow or Bad Payers

Don't keep doing work if a customer does not pay. Ask them to pay if they need something more from you – remind them that your business works just like theirs. It runs on money. If they can't pay for everything, get them to pay something or make a promise that they will stick to.

Credit check your customers – regularly, not just when you first start doing business with them. Things change, and even good customers can get in trouble from time to time. Try not to allow them to make their problem yours. Sign up to a good credit reference agency. Most will send you updates when your customers' credit scores change. It's cheaper than a bad debt, and at least the cost is expected. Unexpected bad debt from a customer can seriously harm your business.

Mechanise and clean up workflows

You don't want to spend your time making sure that invoices go out on time, that deliveries happen, and all the other day-to-day tasks that are so necessary to make a sale happen. As far as possible, you want these tasks to happen automatically and seamlessly. Without that, you will always be wasting time and putting out fires, and it will be very difficult for your business to grow.

The good news is that most cloud-based accounting packages are great at this. With a little time invested at the beginning, you can get regular invoices going out automatically, emails chasing non-paying customers, and so on.

But the accounting takes place after you have made the sale and produced and delivered the goods or services. You need to record your workflows to ensure that this happens in a consistent way every time, so that you can populate your accounts package, get the invoice out and get paid. This process starts with taking on a new customer or getting a new order. Ask yourself - How do you get your product or service sold and to the customer? Who does it? When? How?

Reflect again on Rudyard Kipling's poem, the **overconfidence** section, and be able to answer all 6 questions. Make sure your team knows what is expected of them, when, how etc. This will enable you to replicate what you do, allow the team to do more, and encourage growth.

There are 5 ways to **scale your business** which also make it easier to run.

Simply put, you need to:

Work out the **workflows**

Work out the procedures to make sure the workflows happen

Organise training so that people follow the procedures

Design a monitoring system and

Set up your reporting system

You are very likely to find ways of automating some of these procedures and even link them with your accounts software to save more human intervention and speed things up. It's worth the investment in time. It's like gardening – plan the layout, plant the seeds, water regularly, keep the weeds down, and enjoy the result.

11

Reports

What reports should you have, and when should you have them?

Below are 2 sets of reports – generic reports (ones that every business should have) and reports specific to your business. When reading them, keep in mind the **relationships and assumptions** and how the **4 rules of bookkeeping work**.

Generic Reports

Profit & Loss Account Year to Date (last month if finalised)	Monthly
compared to previous Year to Date	
Last month compared to previous year	Monthly
Balance Sheet last month compared to previous	Monthly

Don't run these reports until you know you have all the invoices etc. in for the month, as they won't make for a sensible comparison with the last period.

(note VAT/Payroll taxes/Corporation Tax amounts and when due)

Aged Debtors	Weekly
Aged Creditors	Weekly
Bank balance	Daily

For reports to be meaningful, you need to update your books daily, or weekly at worst. If you have a feed direct from your bank into your accounting software this does a lot of the work for you. See **Mechanise**.

Business Specific Reports:

Sales per customer (This Year and Last Year)	Monthly
Margin per customer	Monthly/quarterly
Sales items (number of items a,b,c etc) and order values	Monthly/quarterly
Sales (so you can monitor against budgets and forecasts)	Daily/weekly

If you have a service business, you might also want to look at utilisation of time and work in progress lock up (unbilled work) as well.

Specifics to look for

Sales

Changes in sales – look for volume changes, remembering that every change is a function of price and volume. Unless you have changed prices, this will be solely a volume change.

Changes in Gross Profit %

But beware, remember that gross profit is sales minus costs of sales. That takes into account the stock you still have. So don't do this simplistic measure of "I've sold £1000 worth and bought £1000 worth of stock, so my gross profit is Nil." It is only if you've sold all £1000 of stock. You need to have some idea of what your stock is worth at any given point in time.

That doesn't mean you have to count stock every month. Neither is it usually helpful to rely completely on any computerised stock control system unless you have physical control over the stock. Physical control means a team member shouldn't be able to take something out of stock without recording it.

For most small businesses, that isn't feasible. You can spend all your time and energy recording things, not selling them. Set up simple stock systems so you can see the stock levels. Maybe clear bins with a Red Amber Green (RAG) rating – lines on the bin, so when it drops below A, you buy more, and you know that (say) 20 items fill it to R, 40 to A and 60 to G. The more visual your system, the better. Perhaps also put photos of the part on the bin and reflect that in your work orders so everyone knows exactly what part to use. No more long part numbers, which are easy to get wrong.

Whilst you want to be forensic in assessing GP%, bear in mind stock movements and your pricing structure. You will have a feel for what is happening and what you need to do about it.

Unexpected Changes in Costs

Some variations can be explained by items being posted in the wrong place or the wrong period. As an example, the rent was due in December but wasn't paid until January and then posted to building repairs and not rent, whereas last year, it was paid in December and posted to rent. A simple adjustment sorted out what, in effect, is 2 variances caused by one mistake.

Keeping things consistent helps a lot in deciding what changes (variances) need investigation. This time, they only had to correct the bookkeeping. There was no need to make any decision except to make sure no time was wasted on this type of mistake if trivial unless the variance showed a trend over several months.

In conclusion, I know that running your own business is tiring, stressful and lonely. I hope this book makes your life that little bit easier and better.